Step-up, Start-up & Stay-up
In Business

Step-up, Start-up & Stay-up
In Business

A guide to the Financial & Legal aspects of
becoming Self-Employed or Starting a Business

Eileen Hirst

authorHOUSE®

AuthorHouse™
1663 Liberty Drive
Bloomington, IN 47403
www.authorhouse.com
Phone: 1-800-839-8640

Published by AuthorHouse   01/11/2013

ISBN: 978-1-4817-8190-9 (sc)
ISBN: 978-1-4817-8191-6 (e)

Contents

Introduction

Are you one of the many people who have a business idea they would love to try out? Would you like to work for yourself in doing something you really enjoy? Or is your job about to disappear and the only way forward for you is to become freelance or self-employed?

Business start-ups are on the increase with more and more people choosing to work for themselves or start their own business ("start-ups") as a substitute, or in addition to, paid employment. From the market or EBay trader to the doctor, the number of people starting-up or having an additional source of income is increasing daily. Some are excited and positive about doing something they have always wanted to do; others are reluctant or fearful of entering into something they know little about, but see it as their only alternative. Starting-up, willingly or reluctantly, can be overwhelming, especially with regard to the financial and legal aspects such as raising and managing money, sorting out tax and national insurance, and complying with the many legal rules and regulations relating to things such as Health & Safety, employment law and so forth. It means getting involved in things that someone else has taken care of before and the thoughts of getting sued or upsetting the tax people can stop people going ahead with a business idea that would in all probability work out well.

This book will give you an overview of these rules and regulations and signpost you to where you can find further help and advice as a start-up. It is an easy to understand guide to the financial and legal implications of starting a business; a foundation in managing these issues and a guide to overcoming the business "jargon" involved in the various form-filling activities, including business plans, which you will have to have if you need to raise money. Marketing is just as important—when you think about it, if you don't get any customers, you don't really need to know about the financial and legal side of things—but it is not included as a subject in this book. You can learn about marketing in "Of Course I

Can!" All you need to know about Marketing for the Self Employed and Start-Up Business.

This book covers the answers to the questions most start-ups ask before they take the plunge, such as; how to register your business, how to raise and manage finance, how to avoid trouble with the tax people, and how to cope with legal issues such as insurance, health and safety, terms and conditions and so forth and it will enable you to understand the basics of business planning so that you can turn your business idea into a business proposition and assess its viability. If you then decide to go ahead, it will show you how to start out legally and remain financially safe. Start-ups who prepare and plan their business venture have double the chance of being successful! There is also help and advice available to you through the banks and government agencies and in the early stages, an overview of the financial and legal side of things definitely makes the difference between success and failure.

If you are uncertain about actually working for yourself, it will give you the information you need to go out and test your business idea. Most importantly, it will show you how to do a "reality check" for a business idea so that you don't embark on a disastrous course which will leave you repaying rent, loans and other debts if your "start-up" doesn't work out initially.

What's different about this book, after all there are plenty of books on starting a business out there already?

When you have read this book you will know how to go about starting a business in a legally and financially "safe" way. Everything is explained simply and clearly and the book covers the main aspects of starting-up that the majority of people feel they need to know about. How do I know this? I know this because I work for myself and part of what I do is training for start-ups in business planning. I have used client feedback to include in this book, the information, like how the tax system works, that they have found most useful and helpful when they were starting-up. Part of my work is with the government's Enterprise Agencies (more of them later) in helping people start-up in business. This book is a summary of the answers to the questions most start-ups ask and can be used to complement any other source of help and advice you may receive.

Do you really need to know so much about business planning if you have a great idea or are just simply working for yourself?

If you want to apply for any grants or loans to help you get started, the answer is "Yes, absolutely Yes!" The government and the economy rely on people starting and maintaining successful businesses which create jobs and contribute to the nation's wealth; in fact society depends on them. Banks are in the business of lending money and have to do so in order to survive themselves, so they also want to help you start-up and survive. But neither the government nor the banks are going to give out or lend money irresponsibly; they need to see a business plan as to what you will do with the money and evaluate the risk of lending it to you; I'm sure you would if it was your money! They will assist you in a variety of ways and you will hear what they have to say later in the book.

Even if you are not looking for finance, business planning doubles your chances of staying and succeeding in business after your start-up period.

What about practical advice rather than just theory?

In the book you will hear from people who have started up and stayed the course in business and self-employment; people who went into business willingly and others who had little choice. Their experiences will help you see that the theory works and is invaluable if you are to stay the course and eventually grow your business.

When you have finished reading this book you will be aware of the pitfalls when starting-up and have the confidence to decide whether or not it's for you; you will also know where to go for help and advice, should you need to. I hope you will feel that you have nothing to lose by developing a basic business plan and testing your idea; do not be put off by the jargon and the legal terminology which will all be explained quite simply. When you have finished reading this book you will be able to go out and have a go, if you choose to do so. As Christine Anne Rowlands says in one of the case studies, from that point, you will learn as you go along. With a sound business proposition and the right advice and training, you will become one of the successful businesses that step-up, start-up and stay-up. Ask for and accept any help and advice you can get from responsible parties; you CAN do this!

Chapter 1

Thinking of starting up in business or becoming self-employed?

If you are reading this book, you probably fall into one of the following categories:

- You have a business idea and would like to try it out
- You've spotted a gap in the market
- You've been made redundant
- Your employer says you have to work on a self-employed or sub-contract basis from now on
- You dislike your job/boss/organisation and see starting-up as an alternative
- You want to work for yourself because it will give you more flexibility, for example, to work around family commitments

These categories all have different implications for start-up businesses. If you had to put them in order of their likelihood of success, how would you rate them?

There is no right answer. Someone with a great idea or someone who has spotted a gap in the market can fail in business because they did not have adequate business skills whilst another with less confidence but the right advice and support can manage to start-up and grow a successful business.

Freedom, status, mission, money and love of what they do have all been claimed to be the driving forces of successful entrepreneurs.

Self-employment is "trending".

In the current economic climate, more and more people are seeing self-employment as an alternative to, or in addition to, employment. Alongside working full or part-time, you can become self-employed or start a business and it is also a great time to "test" a business idea. Redundancies in the private and public sectors have grown in the recession and employers are increasingly looking to take on part-time and self-employed people, giving them more flexibility in uncertain economic conditions. If you think you have a good business idea or would like to work for yourself rather than an employer, information from the Office of National Statistics (ONS) show that this way of working is indeed the current trend:

- The number of people in self-employment in December 2011 was 4.1 million, a 20 year high
- In 2011, a record 400,000 companies were formed

How many businesses fail and why?

The same statistics show that 40% of new businesses fail in the first twelve months and "The Times 100" reports that 1 in 3 businesses fail within 3 years. Why then do so many start-up businesses run into difficulties and cease to operate in such a small space of time? According to market research (Business Information Factsheets: Common Reasons Why Businesses Fail) it is because of the following:

- Insufficient demand in the market for the product or service
- Little or no start-up advice or training
- Lack of planning; business plans double the likelihood of success!
- Financial difficulties including lack of start-up capital, cash flow problems and poor debtor control
- Management and personal issues such as lack of business experience, performance monitoring, data security and health and personal problems
- Little or no results from marketing

Market Research

Before starting up officially, you should undertake market research into your business idea which will give you the answer to the question: "Who cares?"

Harsh but true, if there are already people out there offering what you are offering and they are good at it, there may not be a gap in the market for you. There must be sufficient demand in the market for your product or service. This means that you must study any competitors and market trends and find out if there is a gap that your offering will fill.

Assuming that after your research you feel confident enough to take the next step in starting up, you need to analyse your skills. You might find that if you plot your personal skills against those required to run a business, they are lacking. For example, tradespeople such as builders, joiners, plumbers and so forth may be qualified and experienced in their trade (as would be professionals such as accountants, teachers, consultants, artists, musicians), yet they may have no idea as to how to run a business. This is when you need to look for help and advice from qualified and experienced business people in developing business skills; the good news is that they can be learned.

Then, of course, there is always the money to consider. The majority of people starting up in today's economic climate will have limited resources, particularly in terms of time and money. There are start-up expenses to consider and then you will need a backdrop of money for the day to day running of any new business. This may mean that you have to look to borrowing as a way to starting up and financing the enterprise in the early stages.

And finally, when everything measures up, that is, the market gap is there, your personal and business skills are finely honed and you have your finances in place, you will need to ask yourself if the business will consistently give you enough money to live on and make your efforts worthwhile; if the return is not enough, you will soon lose heart. This is what a business plan will show; it takes into account the market and your predicted performance and profitability in it and will guide and motivate you (and mean that your chances of success will be doubled).

How is self-employment different from employment?

The main difference between working for yourself and working for an employer is centred on the concept of "responsibility".

If you are employed, generally speaking your employer takes responsibility for you; he or she pays your wages, collects and pays your taxes, makes sure the business operates safely and legally, and attracts enough customers to cover the expenses, ultimately keeping everyone, including the owner, profitably employed. As businesses grow and employ people, they develop structures around the business and specialists become responsible for the main functions of the organisation including sales and marketing, finance, personnel, purchasing and administration.

For start-up businesses there is no such structure. The owner has to do everything themself, albeit often with help from family and friends, but ultimately they are responsible for it all. This is why many people see setting up in business as high risk, even though they would love to try it; others are fearless and just do it.

Where to get start-up help and advice: Enterprise Agencies &Banks

People with a business idea, sub-contractors, or the self-employed will usually approach their local Enterprise Agency or a Bank for help when starting out; visit <u>www.nationalenterprisenetwork.org</u> to find your local agency if you do not already know where it is. Enterprise Agencies have Business Advisers and Managers specialising in start-ups and they usually direct people to workshops and one-to-one advice sessions in which they are given help with their business idea, particularly in terms of learning how to develop a business plan. Where start-ups are looking for grants or loans, the finance provider will always want to see a business plan.

Lenders need to see a plan of what people are going to do with their money; they want assurance that they will get it back, with interest. Government bodies need the same information and the same assurance before they will give out grants. Without a business plan there is nothing for them to make a judgement on; no evidence of research into the market, the competition, the finances and the legal provisions.

The government agencies and banks provide excellent advice and training for start-ups. Even if they cannot offer you finance they will help you in other ways. By using their services you will receive help in creating a business plan which you now know will double your chance of success in your venture.

Along with this, you will meet other people who can help you to move your idea on; you will be signposted towards activities and products and services which will support both you and your business and you will meet other people like yourself. Seeking help and advice and joining business networks gives you confidence and the inspiration you need when embarking on something different and new.

Chapter 2

What sort of business should you start; how do you register your business and how does the tax system work?

HMRC (Her Majesty's Revenue & Customs)—The Tax People

If you take money from people for work you have done for them or goods you have sold to them, you have a potential tax liability. When you are employed, your employer calculates the tax and national insurance due to the government on the wages paid to you and deducts it from you weekly or monthly. They then send it to the tax people on your behalf. The government department dealing with tax in the United Kingdom is "HMRC" (Her Majesty's Revenue & Customs); you can visit their website at www.hmrc.gov which contains a massive amount of information. When you work for yourself, it is your responsibility to collect and save your own tax and national insurance and to pay it to HMRC when it is due.

What sort of business should I set up?

There are a variety of business models or "legal business formats" for you to choose from when you start up, all of which are regulated by HMRC.

They are as follows:

- **Sole Trader**
- **Partnership**
- **Limited Company**
- **Social Enterprise**

Each legal format is different and you will have to choose which one is most appropriate for you. The information below will help you do this.

Sole Trader

The simplest way to start up is as a Sole Trader. This term covers self-employed people, sub-contractors and the owner/managers of start-up businesses. The system used by HMRC for collecting taxes from sole traders is known as "Self-Assessment".

Starting up as a Sole Trader has many advantages:

- It is easy and free to register your business
- It is comparatively simple in terms of paperwork and you do not have to have an accountant (although you may choose to have one) which will save you money
- It is easy to get into and out of if your idea does not come to fruition
- It suits part-time businesses and sub-contractors and can be easily combined with employment, full or part-time
- When the business grows you can become a limited company if it benefits you

Partnerships

Where two or more people work together in the same business, they often become a Partnership. Partnerships pay taxes to HMRC in the same way as Sole Traders, through the self-assessment system. It is easy to set up, you do not have to have an accountant but you should have a legal partnership agreement which states the agreed responsibilities of the partners and agrees the terms of operation.

Limited Companies

Limited Companies are another legal structure for start-up businesses and the self-employed. Company taxes are also collected by HMRC but are calculated in a different way from self-assessment, often benefitting growth businesses.

A limited company is a separate legal entity or being, which can sue or be sued (taken to court if things go wrong). It is a body or person in the eyes of the law, just like you or me.

When you buy a limited company, you become the director of the company and as such, you have certain legal obligations. Company accounts have to be filed annually through Companies House (visit www.companieshouse.gov.uk) and you will need an accountant to audit them to show that they give a true and fair view of the company's position. The accountant will also add reports of shareholders and annual general meetings to your financial accounts and show that everything has been done legally.

Certain aspects of the accounts of limited companies can be looked at by anyone on payment of a small fee; this makes the filing system much more "transparent" than self-assessment.

Social Enterprises

"Social Enterprises" are similar to limited companies in the way they are formed but are specialist in nature, usually formed for not for profit community enterprises. They also need to have an accountant to file their annual returns and the directors have strict responsibilities pertaining to the nature of the venture. Visit www.gov.uk for information on how to set up a social enterprise.

Becoming a Sole Trader: Registering; self-assessment; tax and national insurance

Registering with HMRC

As mentioned earlier, as soon as you start to take money from someone you have done work for or have sold things to you have a potential tax liability and must inform HMRC. You have three months to tell them; if you do not tell them within three months you will be fined, the current "penalty" being £100.

To register with HMRC, you can use the website below or telephone them (look in your local telephone directory for the number) or you can call into your local tax office.

Most people will register online so we will go through the online process here; if you register by phone or in person, you will need to provide the same information.

Registering online

Go to the website www.hmrc.gov.uk and click on Self-Assessment. Before you can register with them you have to apply for a unique taxpayer reference number and then wait several days to receive it. When you receive it, go back online and register. The information they require initially is your name, address and National Insurance number, so that bit is easy.

After that you will have to consider paying the first of the taxes for the self-employed; Class 2 National Insurance. Different names for taxes and national insurance are confusing for most people starting out on their own. The easiest way to think about them is to consider all of them taxes; i.e. money you pay to the government via HMRC. The names are historical and do not mean anything to you from a business perspective; it's more about how much they are so you can set aside the money.

Class 2 National Insurance is paid weekly; for 2012/13 it is £2.65 per week. It entitles you to benefits and contributes towards your state pension, so it is important.

Not everyone needs to pay Class 2 National Insurance though, and when registering, you can tick a box to be exempt from it. For safety, if you are unsure, it is better to agree to pay it.

Reasons for asking to be exempt may be as follows:

- If you are already working for an employer and he is deducting Class 1 National Insurance from your wages you may be paying enough already
- If yours is a lifestyle or "hobby" business, maybe just a few sales of things you have made on E-Bay, and you do not expect to make profits above a certain level; in 2012/13 this is £5,595
- If you are nearing state pension age and have paid National Insurance all of your working life, you may have paid enough. You can ask for a forecast online.

When you have completed this process, you have informed HMRC and your legal obligation at the start of your business has been fulfilled.

Self-Assessment

After the registration process you will not hear from the tax office until April the following year, when a self-assessment return will be sent to you.

On this return, sole traders state their "**sales**", any money they have received from people they worked for or customers they sold goods to, and their "**businesses expenses**" such as the cost of stock they bought and business bills they paid such as rent, telephone, advertising and motor expenses (more of this later).

Tax for sole traders is calculated on **profit** (sales less business expenses) after their personal annual tax free allowance has been taken deducted. This means that people who work for themselves have an advantage over employed people in that they are able to claim certain business expenses before they are taxed.

Sole traders pay their taxes in two annual instalments which are due on the 31st January and 31st July each year. They do not pay monthly or weekly as employed people do.

This means that self-employed people need to be able to estimate how much tax and national insurance they owe at any time, and set it aside for the tax bill, when it arrives.

One of the main reasons start-up businesses fail is because they run out of cash to pay their debts. HMRC sends you regular assessments when you make a profit and as with any supplier, they have to be paid, so you need to know how much money to set aside for them.

Often people will advise you to get an accountant as soon as you start. It is true that a good accountant can save you money (by reducing your tax bill) but you must remember that they charge; watching your money is very important when you start a business. If you can understand the basics of the tax system from this book, it will be easier for you to know how much you should be saving for your taxes as you go along. If it is not something you feel is within your particular skill range, it is still worth reading about as it is important that you understand what is happening to you financially when you work for yourself. Many start-ups don't pay a lot of tax initially. Until they become established and their sales take off, many start-ups and sub-contractors get tax refunds in the early years. Understanding how the system works will take the pressure of the taxman away and allow you to concentrate on running your business.

Year End

For many start-up businesses, the first self-assessment return is easy to complete, providing you have kept records of any money you have taken from customers for sales and any business expenses you have paid out.

For the tax year 2012/13, if your sales are below £68,000, as well as declaring your personal information, you only need to complete a "three-line account" on the self-assessment return. The three lines are:

SALES

EXPENSES

PROFIT/LOSS

Note: It is very important when you start out in business to remember these three lines; we will come back to them regularly in the remainder of the book. The above statement is a "magic formula" which will help you be successful in business (as well as being the information you need to complete your tax return).

People are always curious about what constitutes a "business expense"; the thought of off-setting your expenses against the tax you pay, is very appealing. Business expenses are any costs you have incurred in making your sales happen and operating your business. They are covered in more detail when we look at book-keeping by which time you will have more knowledge of how the tax system works. Until then, keep any business receipts you get and start to note down in a diary your business car mileage or travel expenses.

Where people are employed and self-employed, they will sometimes have paid tax and national insurance on their employed work. A P60 is issued by their employer at year end in April and the business profit or loss is combined with these earnings on the self-assessment return. An adjustment is then made by HMRC who send out a revised statement showing a re-calculated figure based on the tax and national insurance you have already paid and what (if anything) is due to them if you made a profit.

Sales over £68000

If the sales for your business are above £68,000 it is still relatively easy to complete your self-assessment return; the only difference is that HMRC expect you to analyse your business expenses under certain headings such as premises, administration, wages, motor expenses, advertising etc. This means that you have to set up a book-keeping system which records your business expenses in categories, giving a more detailed breakdown of what you are claiming.

When the sales of a business reach between £70,000 and £80,000 in any one year, the business is likely to become a "growth" business and the government will be more interested in you; not only are you likely to employ people, which is great for the economy, you are also getting close to the VAT threshold which means that you will probably bring them in more tax revenue. We'll come to VAT soon.

For many start-up businesses making sales of over £68,000 in the first year is unlikely and if this is you, focus on getting customers rather than worrying about growing the business until it becomes likely. You can get help when you grow your business and you will have become more used to keeping records by then.

Setting aside money for your Tax and National Insurance

When you start your business, become self-employed or sub-contract, you will not pay tax for a long time. If you start in May for example, you will not get a self-assessment return until April the following year, eleven months later. If you owe any tax it will not become payable until the end of the following January, twenty months after you started. This is a long time and if you have not done anything with your book-keeping during the first year, how will you know how much money you are going to have to pay in tax and national insurance? Supposing you have done really well and when you eventually get together your figures, you have made a sizeable profit, you will be faced with a tax bill which could leave you in a mess; in fact you could be one of the many who go out of business because they have not set aside enough money to pay their tax bill.

So you have to know, however vaguely, how tax is calculated so that if you are making a profit, you also set aside money for any tax you will have to pay on it. HMRC will do the calculation for you if you send your return in on time, but you will have been trading for over a year by this time and if you have not saved along the way, you will have to find the amount due very quickly. If you know how the tax and national insurance system for businesses works, you can be prepared by setting aside money on a regular basis. You can get interest on this money whilst you are waiting to pay your first bill and it therefore makes good business sense to set it aside as you go along. Most business people who have failed in a previous attempt at business and have started up again, set aside a proportion of their sales money regularly (often 25% as mentioned elsewhere) to cover their HMRC dues—they have been caught out once and they ensure it does not happen a second time.

How tax and national insurance is calculated

Everyone in this country is entitled to a "Personal Allowance". This is the annual amount of money anyone can earn without paying tax or national insurance. For the tax year April 2013/14 it is set at £9205.

When you are employed, your employer will give you a portion of this allowance each payday (weekly or monthly) before calculating your tax and national insurance. When you go it alone, your tax bill is calculated annually. Your annual personal allowance is taken away from your annual profit, and tax is charged on the remainder. For example, if your profit for the year is £15,000, you will deduct £9205 (your annual personal allowance) from it before you calculate tax on the remaining £5795. If your business has had a slow start, or if it is a lifestyle or hobby business and your profit is less than £9205, you will not owe any tax and if you have actually made a loss, you may be able to carry it forward to the next tax year.

After taking away your personal allowance, the remainder of your profit is taxable. There are various rates of tax and they change from time to time in the budget. For most sole traders, the basic rate of tax, 20%, is the one you are likely to pay. It does not increase to 40% until your profit after the personal allowance is higher than £32,010 and most growing businesses will have seen an accountant by then and probably have been advised to become a limited company which has a completely different tax structure.

Now for the big things you will have to watch out for!

There is another tax on profit for sole traders. In addition to Class 2 National Insurance, you may be liable for Class 4 National Insurance (another tax but traditionally classed as National Insurance). Class 4 National Insurance is currently set at 9% of taxable profit. This means that you are now paying tax on profits, after your personal allowance has been deducted, at 29% in total and setting aside 20% is not enough.

If this shocks you or seems unfair, another way to think about it is to look at the amount of National Insurance employed people pay; they pay much more than the £2.65 per week Class 2 contribution, and it is important to remember that Class 4 National Insurance only becomes payable when you make a profit. For many start-up businesses it will not be a huge amount of money initially and you will get used to setting aside the money as your business moves forward.

Paying your tax and national insurance

There is however another thing you need to be aware of with regard to paying your taxes based on annual profit.

As stated at the beginning of this section, when you start your business you will not pay tax for a long time; up to 20 months for May start-ups. Obviously employed people pay their tax and national insurance regularly (PAYE is "Pay As You Earn") and after your first tax bill, HMRC expect you to pay something up front for the year ahead, a "payment on account". Here is an example of how these payments are calculated:

Tax is paid twice a year (or in two instalments). If, after year end in April, the tax for your first year in business is calculated to be say, £2000, you will pay £1000 on January 31st and £1000 on July 31st of the following year. However, as you are now being taxed annually, HMRC want you to start paying some in advance for the next year and ask for a 50% payment, based on your first tax bill, for the following year. This means that they want another £1000 from you and they want it paying with your first instalment, i.e. £2000 becomes payable on the 31st January (£1000 for your first instalment and £1000 representing 50% of your annual tax bill as a payment on account).

You may need to read the previous paragraph several times until you get your head around it; payments on account are confusing. The good thing is that it is really only the first one that you need to be ready for, as in subsequent years it is adjusted up or down according to your increased or decreased profit and you are more prepared for it.

It's easy to see now why people starting out in business get into trouble with the tax people isn't it? Being prepared by setting aside money is essential and when you save money for your taxes, you can get interest on it which belongs to you; a bonus! There is a ready reckoner on the website to help you forecast your tax liability or a simple way would be to ignore the personal allowance etc. and set aside 25% of your **sales** money, from the very start of your business. Whilst this is not exact, it would get you into the habit of setting aside money as it comes in and should be adequate in the first year of your business.

A final word of warning to those who are going to remain employed or part-time employed whilst they start their own business. Your employer may be giving you your personal allowance through the PAYE system and so you will have used some, if not all of it, and may be liable for the full 29% plus a payment on account right from the outset.

Partnerships

Quite often two or more people decide to get together and work in business on a partnership basis. There are many advantages to working in partnership in terms of sharing workloads and experience and it is often attractive because of the flexibility in sharing that it gives to people who have personal commitments which mean they cannot give a business their full attention.

Registering with HMRC

The system for registration with HMRC is the same as for Sole Traders. Both or all partners will register separately with HMRC and then register the business as a partnership. It can be done online and the system is the same as for a sole trader.

Partnership Agreements

There are some pitfalls of working as a partnership that you need to prepare for in advance. Often partnerships are not forever; not because the people argue or don't get on together, often it is because circumstances change and it no longer fits with the business model. People are tempted by the idea of two personal allowances being applied before tax is calculated and often forget that instead of the business paying a wage for one person, two or more people have to live on the annual profit; this means sales have to be much higher in a partnership than for a sole trader.

In a partnership, if a partner dies, the partnership bank account will be frozen. Similarly, if a partner becomes bankrupt, the bank account will have to be closed. Although we never expect this to happen in our business, it needs to be taken into consideration at the outset and all eventualities prepared for in advance.

Partnerships can be very effective business models as long as there is a "Partnership Agreement" in place—a legal document setting out how certain things will be dealt with in the business.

There are several areas that commonly lead to disputes which need to be covered in the agreement including: interest paid on capital introduced into the business; drawings (money each partner takes out as wages) and any interest charged on them; dissolution of the partnership; anything else pertinent to the particular partnership which needs addressing legally.

Any legal agreement needs to be checked by a solicitor to make sure it would stand up in court if there were any subsequent disputes. Legal advice is expensive for start-up businesses and any preparation you can do in advance will save you money. Download a sample partnership agreement and try to adapt it for your partnership before taking it to the solicitor. Not only will you feel more confident about what you are agreeing on, you will save money whilst the clock is ticking off expensive billing hours in the solicitor's office.

Self-Assessment and Year End Returns for Partnerships

Again the system is the same as for a sole trader in that a self-assessment return is submitted to HMRC in April each year. A partnership return will have the combined sales and expenses of all the partners and the personal allowances for each of the partners will be deducted before any tax and Class 4 National Insurance is calculated.

Limited Companies

Registering with HMRC

Many people think they would like to be, or have to be, a company to start a business. We do so much online now and people looking to start a business are likely to come across company formation sites offering their services, including a company name, from just £20 including VAT.

It is as simple as that to buy a limited company; you have to choose a name that has not already been taken, pay the money and you have a company. Companies are listed on the Companies House website www. companieshouse.co.uk and providing the name you want is available, you can be the owner of a limited company in minutes.

Just stop for a minute before you press the "Buy" button though and check that it is the most appropriate way to start your business. We'll start by looking at limited companies as business models and then look at their advantages and disadvantages for start-ups.

Limited Liability

A limited company is a separate legal entity or being, which can sue or be sued (taken to court if things go wrong). It is a body or person in the eyes of the law, just like you or me.

When you buy a limited company, you become the director of the company and as such, you have certain legal obligations. Company accounts have to be filed annually through Companies House and you will need an accountant to audit them; to show that they give a true and fair view of the company's position. The accountant will also add reports of shareholders' and annual general meetings to your financial accounts to show that everything has been done legally.

Many people are attracted to the limited company model because of "limited liability". As a company is a separate legal body, if it is unable to pay its bills, any creditor (person or business the company owes money to) will sue the company or take the company to court to recover the debt. This is what limited liability is about; the director is not personally involved if he or she has carried out their director's duties properly. If the company loses in court, it can be declared bankrupt and its assets (the things it owns) can be seized by the creditor (quite often this will be HMRC).

Obviously this looks like a great advantage; people imagine themselves as directors who can walk away from the company when things go wrong and still retain their own personal assets. It is not surprising that people become limited companies when they start out without looking at it more closely, as it appears very attractive.

Let's consider some of the things about limited companies that may not be as advantageous to a start-up business as they appear at first glance.

With regard to limited liability and borrowing money, in practice, banks and investors will not lend you money just because you have a limited company. They need you to offer them some sort of security against any money they lend you in case you cannot meet the repayments and a new company without assets (things that it owns) does not offer them this security. If your company has a building or it owns a fleet of vehicles, then they may be willing to lend against those assets. If not they will almost certainly ask you for a personal guarantee; a loan secured against your own assets, for example, your home. If therefore, as a start-up, you have bought a limited company for the protection limited liability gives you and your company has no assets to guarantee repayment of any loans, you will not have benefitted.

An accountant will charge you a minimum of £500 +VAT, therefore £600 to complete a set of limited company accounts, and £500 is the minimum; many firms will charge you more. Your accountancy fees are genuine business expenses and you can put them through your books. But is committing to £600 not a total luxury for someone who is just starting out in business and is not even sure that they will get enough customers to make a go of it at this stage?

When you commit to a fixed cost, such as an accountant's annual fee for a set of company accounts, you have to pay it whether you make a profit or not. You could certainly use £600 in some other way as a start-up business and if you start off as a sole trader, you can do your own self-assessment, or get that Auntie or friend to help you; an accountant is much less expensive for self-assessment than for a limited company.

You can move from being a sole trader to a limited company at any time. As your business progresses and acquires assets, having a company which holds these assets will allow banks and investors to consider lending to you and most successful start-ups do tend to become limited companies in time. At the start though, do not become a limited company unless it will benefit you in some way; you can buy a limited company and leave it dormant until you grow as a sole trader if you really want one but as soon as you trade through it you will be subject to more cost and bureaucracy.

Other reasons for forming a company

Some start-up businesses may need to become a limited company in order to be considered for contracts with potential customers. For example, some public and local authorities and some of the large corporations expect businesses which tender for work with them to be limited companies. This is because limited companies are much more "transparent" than sole traders.

If you have a limited company your accounts are published on the Companies House website annually and anyone can access them. Your company history is recorded and is available to the public for a small fee. Self-assessment is very different; you are amongst millions of people sending information directly to HMRC and it remains private.

If you have to have a limited company in order to get work, then so be it. On the plus side, a limited company can portray a bigger image from a marketing point of view, but bear in mind the increase in bureaucracy in terms of returns to complete, and the fact that you will be legally responsible for the actions of the company as the director.

Filing Accounts at Year End

Limited companies do not have to file their accounts with Companies House in April as they can choose their own year-end date, usually a year after start-up; many still choose to use April to stay in line with the government tax year.

For small companies HMRC need the same information as for sole traders; sales, expenses (broken down into categories) and profit or loss. There are however, differences in the way company taxation is calculated.

Calculating Tax & National Insurance for Limited Companies

Calculating tax for limited companies is more complicated than for sole traders. Recent legislation has meant that the rate of (corporation) tax for small limited companies is set at the same rate as for a sole trader, currently 20%. There is no Class 4 National Insurance involved but as the director is classed as an employee of the company, tax and national insurance above a certain income level will be deducted from his or her wages on a PAYE basis and the company may have to pay Employers National Insurance (currently 13.8%) for them. After corporation tax has been charged on profits, the remainder can be distributed as "dividends" to directors and any other shareholders.

As limited companies have to use an accountant, start-up businesses can take advice immediately as to how to set out their book-keeping (it will not be significantly different from that of a sole trader at the outset) and how much to set aside for tax.

Generally speaking, it is simpler to start out as a sole trader and see an accountant when you feel your business has taken off and is likely to grow—often when it looks as if you are going to reach that £70,000 to £80,000 Sales figure. Many people do however take the plunge from the word "Go!" and start out as a limited company with a goal to grow the business as soon as possible. Your personal vision and goals will obviously determine how you want to proceed with your business and there is no right or wrong way, just as long as you play by HMRC's rules.

Social Enterprises

Social Enterprises are usually set up for community based businesses. For example, where a village has been awarded lottery funding and a legal structure needs to be put in place to protect and regulate the members of the committee in organising and using the finances and operating in a legal manner, the people involved are likely to look at the social enterprise model.

The accounts process is similar to that of a limited company; accounts are submitted to HMRC and an accountant is required from the outset so it is better to find one who specialises in social enterprises.

As with a company, there are directors and they may be paid a director's "remuneration" or salary. Unlike a company however, profits remain within the social enterprise; wages are paid to directors in accordance with what is agreed in the formal documentation and approved by the board at their meetings.

Are there any other taxes?

Value Added Tax (VAT)

This tax is a business tax and applies to any type of business whatever the legal format or status with sales of £77,000 and over (known as the VAT Threshold).

Registering for VAT

The VAT Threshold is set each year in the budget at a certain level of sales (**not profit**) currently £77,000. This means that when your business sales look as though they are going to reach the threshold in one year, you must register with HMRC for VAT. Certain businesses are exempt from VAT; generally speaking this is where the business sells essential products such as food or medicine or offers essential services such as nursing care. It is easy to check with HMRC if you are unsure as to whether or not VAT applies to your business sector.

How the VAT system works

From the date the business is registered for VAT, 20% of the sales of the business must be paid at regular intervals (often monthly or quarterly) to HMRC. Any VAT the business pays out for stock or expenses can be reclaimed against this but as the sales of a business are more than its expenses, most businesses will end up paying a net difference to HMRC after registration. Start-ups selling products, online or market traders for example, are likely to reach the threshold sooner than those selling services because of the high sales turnover.

Will VAT affect my start-up?

Start-ups should monitor their sales closely as they will not be able to suddenly increase their prices because they have reached the VAT threshold and have to charge it. Customers can always go to competitors with lower prices (including other start-ups who have not yet reached the threshold) and will do unless they get something in return for the price increase. If your business looks likely to reach £77,000 in sales in its first year of trading, the best strategy is to increase prices gradually before registration and as your customers become established and loyal. Although VAT on sales is high at 20%, there is VAT to be reclaimed on stock and expenses, so registration often means that the business will pay HMRC a far lower figure than 20% of their sales.

Completing a VAT Return

Becoming VAT registered is a growth step for any business and as stated earlier, when your business grows to around £70k to £80k in sales, it is advisable to see an accountant, if you have not already done so. Your book-keeping may have to be adjusted so that you can complete a VAT Return easily and there are various schemes whereby small businesses can pay a set percentage of sales income to cover their VAT liability, rather than establishing a new and more time consuming recording system. HMRC run free workshops on VAT registration and you can book online for them.

Reaching the VAT threshold is a more significant step for businesses selling to the public, rather than those selling to other businesses. Often other businesses you sell to will be registered for VAT too and they can reclaim any VAT you charge them and will not be affected if you have to start adding it to their invoices. The general public have no way of reclaiming it though and will see it as an increase in prices, which is why you need to plan for its introduction before you reach the threshold.

Case Studies: Andrew Makin & Val Holmes

Self-employment—Beyond the theory

From the statistics on recent start-ups, it is clear that self-employment is growing, yet not everyone who sets out in business does it willingly. Many people would prefer a more financially secure way of life and self-employment has been the last resort for them. Let's look at two people who are currently working for themselves and how they view it.

Self-employed subcontractor: Andrew Makin

Andrew, who is qualified and time-served in carpentry and joinery, has worked on a self-employed and sub-contracting basis in the construction industry for the past nine years. He stresses that it is not his choice; he became a sub-contractor when the building companies in the North of England changed the way they employed trades people during the building boom and in the subsequent recession. Because the UK construction sector is dominated by small firms and demand for construction is location and project based, building contractors in his area tend to hire local sub-contractors rather than employing trades people; employment is often not an option, as in Andrew's case.

When he set out on a self-employed footing, he went into his local tax office and asked for help and advice and they sorted everything out for him then and there; he knows that things have changed since then and because of the large number of people who become self-employed, the emphasis is centred more on providing free of charge short training courses than on one-to-one help.

At the end of the tax year and each year since, he has used an accountant to complete his tax return. He has recently changed his accountant to one recommended by colleagues and says that it has saved him money in that he has not paid as much tax. He keeps payment slips from the contractors, records his travel expenses and keeps any receipts for tools and passes them to the accountant who completes his self-assessment return for him. This year he paid his accountant £250 plus VAT and although he knows that others offer lower fees, he thinks that using someone recommended through word of mouth is better than going for the lower priced options as a good accountant will ensure you pay the right amount of tax, and only that amount.

He does not think that self-employment is an easy route. The thing he finds most difficult is the fact that the work can finish at a moment's notice as there are currently no contracts in place—trades people are "laid off" regularly, especially in winter. Work tends to be seasonal; it often finishes in the run up to Christmas and does not start again until well into the New Year, weather permitting. He is personally responsible for buying and running his van and paying the insurance for it; including the cost of carrying tools, this is around £700 per annum. As he is not paid holiday pay or sick pay, he has considered taking out private insurance but has found it to be both limiting in what it covers, and expensive.

Andrew is one of the many self-employed people in the construction industry who would prefer to be employed but the fragmentation of the construction industry and the domination of small firms in his local area has made it impossible for him to find a permanent position.

Val Holmes: Business Advisor, Trainer & Beauty Therapist

Val was employed by a national newspaper group for 25 years and worked her way up to the Northern Classified Advertisement Manager, managing a team of 40 staff across the North of England. She then left to start her own business. With a degree in Marketing, which she completed whilst working for the newspaper group, she started up as a sole trader specialising in training in sales & marketing and initially gained a contract, lecturing for a Further Education College part-time day and evening. She also worked during the day as a Marketing Consultant on contracts for local business organisations. She then became a qualified Business Adviser and Mentor, supporting people who were starting up in business.

All went well until the funding for the organisations she was working with came to an end and not all of the training providers were given further contracts; this meant that when an organisation lost a contract, Val often did too. She found, like Andrew that work was sporadic; contracts were available sometimes, but even then, they were for very limited timescales. She finally reached the point where she missed the security of employment and applied for a position as the Media Co-ordinator for five Further Education Colleges and Universities which involved developing media training to industry, particularly in the light of the imminent move of the BBC to Salford Quays in 2012.

On completion of the media project Val was asked to stay on and work in the Business Department to develop and deliver business skills training to industry. During this time she was approached by a Business Support organisation who offered her a self-employed contract with very good terms. She had worked for them previously and after careful thought, decided she would embark on the self-employed route once again. She had enjoyed the regular salary but found that she missed the flexibility and variety that self-employment had given her. Also whilst watching and helping other women set up their businesses, Val realised that she would like to become involved in the holistic therapy and beauty business herself, so at the same time as she took the contract for the Business Advisor and Trainer position, she enrolled on an evening course for therapy and sports massage.

When her business support contract ended in 2011, she decided to change course completely and focus on the holistic and beauty therapy business. She loved the work and realised that she would have more control over her future income by adding other streams to the portfolio of services she could offer. Armed with fliers, she set out in her free time to visit care homes, hotels, spas and beauty salons in her area, offering her services.

She now works on a self-employed basis both as a Business Trainer and a Holistic/Beauty Therapist. She is employed on a part-time basis four days each week with a national hotel chain in their beauty spa, and she also works on a self-employed basis for a training company.

Because of her business knowledge and skills, working for herself has not been difficult. Val keeps her own books but does employ an accountant at year end. It has taken a long time and she has had a lot of ups and downs but is now in a position where she is comfortable with the financial aspects of her income and is doing what she loves. She has the flexibility and variety she needs and having multiple streams of income has given her the financial peace of mind she needed along with the contentment of doing something she loves.

Chapter 3

Book-keeping: Recording Business Transactions

Whichever business format you choose, you will need to start immediately to keep records of your transactions, not only for compiling your year-end accounts, but also to monitor how your business is performing.

Organising pieces of paper, writing figures into books or inputting them onto spread sheets is decidedly unfashionable in today's hi-tech world, but it is essential from a business perspective. As with marketing, if you fail to get feedback and don't constantly review and alter direction accordingly, you will go off course, lose control of your position and where you are heading for. Book-keeping records give you feedback on progress and allow you to produce accounts which help you plan your future direction.

Start-up expenses

When you start-up you should make a list any items you have bought or are introducing into the business, as their value can be claimed as start-up expense. For example, a joiner or builder will have tools and equipment which they bring into their business when they set up; hairdressers will have products and equipment and consultants will have laptops, stationery and software which they will use too. As well as items bought specifically for the business at start-up, these can be introduced into the business at the current market value on commencement of the business (search for the present value of items on auction internet sites if you are unsure of the value). Anything you buy or already have which is going to be used in the business should be listed with its cost or market value and the total sum is your investment into the business, along with any cash you may introduce. An Annual Investment Allowance figure which covers set-up costs is set by HMRC each year for new businesses to take advantage of; value up to this amount may be claimed in the first year as a tax deductible expense in its entirety.

Recording sales income and business expenses

It is easy to keep basic, on-going book-keeping records. At the simplest level, you just need to record any money that comes into your business and any that you pay out. If you have ever done a car boot sale you will be able to imagine how this works:

When you get home from the sale you immediately empty your pockets and count the money you have taken. These "takings" are your sales income or "sales revenue" in book-keeping terms. Every day, or at least most days, a business has takings and all you have to do is add them up and record them in writing, or input them into your accounting system, noting the date and the amount of money you took.

It's the same for your business expenses. Each day, empty your pockets and take out receipts for any items you have paid for which were necessary for you to operate your business. With the car boot sale, you had your travel costs, an entrance fee, a couple of cups of coffee whilst you were there and the cost value of the goods or "stock" that you sold (you can't include the value of any stock that you took but did not sell).

As stated earlier, with regard to tax, it is always better to get a receipt when you incur an expense; the receipt is evidence of payment if ever there is a dispute. However, at the car boot sale, it is unlikely that you would have been given receipts for any money you spent, so what do you do? HMRC should allow any fair and reasonable expenses relating to your business to be deducted from your sales income before any tax is calculated, so after you have entered your takings, you should work out your expenses, even those with no receipt, and record them on a separate sheet. Let's look at them.

You paid the entrance fee (even though you probably weren't given a receipt) so that's the first entry; the date and the amount, very straightforward. The remaining expenses are not as straightforward.

Motor vehicle expenses

With regard to the travel or cost of getting to and from the sale, unless your travel was by bus or train and you have a receipt, you will need to record your business mileage as it can be claimed as an expense. If you are a regular trader and have a vehicle which is used only for business, in this case for selling at car boot sales, recording individual journeys is not necessary as all the costs of using the vehicle are tax deductible. Business mileage logs are required where you use a private vehicle for both personal and business use. You have to extract the business cost of using the vehicle from the total cost, for inclusion in your accounts.

Your business mileage log is essential and easy to keep once you get into the habit. You can leave a small pad or book in your vehicle and jot down the number of business miles you do each day; the date, where you went and the number of miles. Each mile you travel for business can be currently (2012/13 tax year) claimed at 45p per mile (this rate changes, usually in the budget) so it is well worth recording. Just to explain this further, it is important to realise that HMRC are not going to pay you 45p per business mile; they are going to allow you to claim the expense against your takings, which means that you will pay less tax if your business makes a profit.

So if your journey to the car boot sale and back was 30 miles, you would be able to claim £13.50 (30x45p) in your expenses, jotted down after the entrance fee as business mileage. There is another way to claim business vehicle expenses which involves keeping all receipts and apportioning them at the end of the year into business and personal mileage costs; either way you need to keep a business mileage log.

Subsistence

Back to the remainder of the car boot sale expenses; what about those two cups of coffee and any food you bought; after all you have no receipt for them? There will always be confusion about certain expenses and whether or not HMRC will view them as acceptable; "subsistence" is one of these expenses. The law is that you can claim for "fair and reasonable" expenses. I was told by an accountant that the tax inspector in my district looked closely at "subsistence" and disallowed high amounts of expenses claimed by some businesses. His view was that people had to eat and drink and it was just the additional cost (in this case the additional cost of the food and drink above what it would have cost you to make at home) that would be claimed. So you have to be fair and reasonable; maybe you could claim 50% of what you paid?

HMRC's treatment of business expenses

With expenses, it is important to remember that the government and its tax officers want you to start a (good) business. They will not intentionally punish you for minor book-keeping errors; you probably would not be sent to prison for the odd slip up, although you would be for being deliberately dishonest. If you list expenses that HMRC do not agree with, they will surcharge you for the amount of tax that you saved by claiming them. You have the right to appeal and at the end of the day it is what would be deemed fair and reasonable in a court of law that counts, so be sensible yet don't be afraid to claim expenses you feel are justifiable. HMRC run workshops on a variety of topics including business expenses and they are very good; look on the website for information about them.

Stock

The final expense of the car boot sale is the cost of stock; the cost price to you of the goods you sold there. If you had "purchased" or bought stock to sell at the car boot sale, you will probably have receipts for it. If it was your own stock, you will have to value it at today's market price and it will be included in your accounts as goods introduced into the business. Either way, the amount will be entered up on the list of expenses as stock with the appropriate amount or value.

Summarising business transactions

So that's it; job done, boring book-keeping completed as below:

Takings/Sales Income/Sales Revenue	£250.00
Expenses:	
Travel (30miles @ 45p)	£13.50
Entrance Fee	£10.00
Subsistence	£2.00
Stock/Goods	£100.00

Calculating profit

By regularly recording your income and expenses, you will be fulfilling your legal requirements and maintaining a record which at the end of the tax year will give you the 3 magic figures for the self-assessment return from HMRC:

Sales   £250.00
Expenses   £125.50
Profit   £124.50

Maintaining records of your incomings and outgoings for yourself is as important as maintaining them for the taxman but many traders are blasé about it:

"I know I'm doing okay because I sold a load of stuff at the car boot sale for £250 which I only paid £100 for! I don't need to write it down, I know what to buy and I'm good at selling it."

You can see that the profit was only really £124.50 not £150.00; not much difference but if you did this with all of your book-keeping transactions, you would have a very inflated idea of how much you were making and you would have less to claim against tax at year end.

Debtors and Creditors

Non-cash businesses regularly have money owing to them from customers or "debtors"; alongside this they will owe money to suppliers and providers of services, their "creditors". They must therefore keep records of what money is due into the business from their debtors and what is due out of the business to their creditors. They do this by recording invoices which they send out to customers and marking them off with the date they are paid. This is known as "credit control". Invoices and payments to creditors are treated in the same manner. From the outstanding balances a clear picture of the true position of the business can be determined.

Cash and bank balances

A daily running total of transactions in cash and through the business bank account should also be maintained. If small cash transactions in or out of the business are unrecorded, they will not be claimed on your tax return and eventually this will mean you pay more tax.

Online banking means that you can check your account daily and this should become routine. It will enable you to avoid bank charges which can arise from late payments from customers or unexpected or unplanned expenses which can result in your account going "into the red" or overdrawn. A personal business banking manager will support you in avoiding this as they know it is a common problem with start-ups. They can organise text alerts and some will even call you themselves if it looks as though there are going to be problems with your bank account.

If you do not use online banking, keep a written record showing the bank balance at the start of the day, adjusted for "ins" and "outs" during the day and giving a closing balance at the end of the day. This type of record can be used for cash transactions too.

Book-keeping systems

If all you do is write down all of your business incomings and out-goings, file the receipts and keep your mileage log, you will cover the essentials necessary to run a business in the early stages.

Spread-sheets & Computerised Accounts Packages

Excel spread sheets are very popular with start-ups and take some of the pain out of bookkeeping as you use formulae to do the calculations; one sheet for sales takings and a sheet for expenses (date; who you paid; amount) will get you started.

Then there are computerised account packages such as Sage and Quick Books which are brilliant, if you can use them. If you are not familiar with them it may take you some time to learn how to use them and you need to ask yourself if that would be the best use of your time at the start of a business. Use a system that suits you and makes the best use of your limited time.

Book-keeping should become a habit with you if you want your business to survive for any length of time. It will help you "cost" jobs or projects so that you ask the right selling prices and it acts as a great guide as to which of the areas of your business are most profitable. This will keep you moving forward and give you the stability to grow the business;

the worst case scenario is leaving it all until the end of the year and then finding out that you haven't made any money. If you really do not want to do the book-keeping then get someone to do it for you, but have regular meetings with them so that you know what's going on. You have enough information now to understand the figures and ask the right questions.

Chapter 4

Raising Finance & Business Bank Accounts

Assessing your financial requirements at start-up

When you are considering your business idea, it is natural to set out a list of the things you need to start-up. Often this will include a van or motor vehicle, premises to operate from and equipment to work with, as well as cash to buy stock and pay for expenses. And it is good to make a list of your **ideal** requirements, even though this list may be just a starting point, a "wish list" of everything you feel you really need to have to start-up with. If you then cost out this list, you will probably find that starting-up in your ideal way is impractical or impossible as you do not have access to enough money.

Start-up businesses need finance, not only to start up with, but also to keep the business running on a day to day basis. Businesses use their sales income to finance the business but this is really only possible once the business is significantly established with regular customers. For start-up businesses, in the beginning, sales income will be slow and/or sporadic, yet there will be expenses to pay out to keep the business going, even if it is only petrol for your car or bus or rail tickets. This means that if you do not have any money of your own or family and friends to support you by giving or loaning you money, you will probably have to approach a lender, if not at the beginning of your business start-up, at some later time as your business takes off.

Where would I go for finance?

Where people have little in the way of personal savings, or friends or family to help them, they will often look to the government for support. Whilst the government does help small businesses to start-up, it does not tend to be with grants, cash or loans, particularly at the "idea" stage of starting a business. Finance for start-ups is particularly difficult to come by and often expensive because of the high risk of failure. Enterprise Agencies and other organisations including the Job Centres are government funded to help people start out in business and generally they are still around to do this, although grants and small loans are limited. As mentioned in the introduction, government agencies now often help by giving advice and organising workshops and training in business skills, particularly in developing a business plan. As the evidence supports the view that start-ups with business plans are significantly more likely to survive, the government continues to provide such services, and links any grants or loans to people who have successfully completed programmes and developed a viable business plan.

Most start-ups will approach a bank for finance if there is no other option in the form of government grants and loans.

Approaching the banks for finance

Whilst there is this valuable government advice and support out there if you search for it, it is still necessary for many start-ups to try to source finance in the form of loans and other methods of credit from the banks.

Margaret Mooring, a local Business Manager for start-ups with Barclays Bank insists that despite what you may hear in the news, there is finance available from the banks. In fact, she says that Barclays have never stopped lending, even throughout the recent "credit crunch".

Here's what she has to say about borrowing from Barclays:

"At Barclays it is business as usual. The bank is lending money to Start-up and existing customers, in fact we have continued to lend throughout the current financial crisis.

For a new business, the bank will need to see a business plan and forecast figures in order to assess the viability and nature of your business. The customer will need to be investing at least the same amount themselves to the amount they are requesting to borrow; in other words matching their stake with the amount of the loan.

Customers can chose a repayment term from one to ten years to suit their budget and can repay early without any penalty.

The interest rate is calculated for each prospect based on the risk involved; a start-up business will generally pay a higher rate than an established business. There will be a set-up fee which is added to the loan and included in the monthly repayments.

A start-up business will need to provide the same information for an overdraft as for a loan application. The arrangement fee for an overdraft is charged monthly in arrears. This will assist the business with their cash flow."

Business Plans

Any potential lender will want to see a plan of what you are going to use the money for, a business plan. Your business plan will be checked against the lender's specific criteria and they will assess the likelihood of getting their money back from you. They will be looking for some form of security from you, just in case it doesn't work out as you have told them. They may even fix the interest rate at a level in accordance with their risk; the higher they view the risk of the business failing, the higher the rate of interest they will charge you. If you think about it another way (which is often what you have to do with things that don't initially seem possible in the business world) if you were the lender, what would you be looking for if you were asked for a loan? You would want to feel pretty sure that the business could repay your loan and you would probably want some interest on it. You would expect its owner to come up with a back-up plan in case things went wrong and he or she could not meet the loan repayments, wouldn't you? These are the things you should consider when compiling your business plan; as well as for your own use, it must be written in a way that reassures the lender and thereby reduces the risk on their part.

Where to go for finance if you are "declined" by a Bank

Start-ups without a track record or acceptable credit history may be unable to access bank finance if they do not fit the criteria requirements.

The government tries to help start-ups who have been declined by the banks providing they have a good business plan which shows a viable business proposition and an ability to repay any finance loaned to them. Let's hear from Margaret about how this works in practice:

"If your lending application isn't initially accepted, don't be concerned. It may just be that at this moment in time your business isn't ready to take on more finance.

Your Barclays Business Manager can advise you on a number of alternative financing options including Enterprise Finance Guarantee (EFG)—which acts as a guarantee for bank loans to SME's that lack the necessary security for the finance they need, or a loan from a Community Development Finance Institution.

Other options include an angel investor group, which can lend you the capital to help your business when it needs it most."

How do I start up if I cannot borrow any money?

You may wonder how anyone gets started in business if they do not have savings or a friend or relative to help them out. The only way is to start in a small way, usually by testing your business idea in whatever way you can. If you can show from this testing that there is a market for your business proposition and it is likely to be successful, a finance provider will look more favourably at your requirements.

Often people just can't get the finance to start in their ideal way. Others cost out their business idea and decide they do not want the commitment and burden of monthly loan repayments, especially when they know it will be difficult to get customers in the early days. At this point—often referred to as the "reality check"—it is important to realise that this may not be the end of your idea, your "dream"; you can often think of a way of starting out in a smaller, more gradual way. For traders, if you can manage initially without buying a van, or leasing premises or buying such a high level of stock, why not test your idea, say on a market stall or E-Bay? In that way, you can develop a business history showing demand and then go to a lender with a plan based on facts and figures, which will certainly be looked on more favourably if there are orders in the pipeline, and particularly if the lender knows that you have also taken advice and attended business courses to help develop your enterprise skills.

Business Bank Accounts

One of the questions people ask when setting up a business is:

"Do I need a business bank account?"

Legally, you do not have to have a business bank account; you can run a business without a bank account, a cash business. Practically, it is better to have a business bank account for the following reasons:

- A business bank account will create a history of transactions which will give you a "credit rating". A good credit rating makes raising finance for your business in the form of loans and overdrafts easier.
- A separate bank account for your business transactions makes keeping your books and records better; everything is in one account and you can use the statements as evidence of incomings and outgoings for tax purposes, particularly if you do not have receipts.
- Because of "money laundering" regulations, bank employees look closely at accounts which have a lot of cash transactions. If they think that you are running a business through a personal account they can close it and insist you open a business one.
- A business bank account gives your start-up more credibility. Your potential customers will see it as a legitimate business and this will offset some of the risk they may feel in dealing with a new business.

How do I get a business bank account and how much will it cost me?

Margaret from Barclays talks us through what happens when she has a request to open a business bank account:

"Legally you do not have to have a business bank account; however it is much better to start as you mean to go on. You will be building a clear business track record for the future and ensuring that you have access to all of the business support and specialist advice which the bank can give you to help you survive and succeed.

You will not be charged for operating a business account for a minimum of one, and maximum of two years. We have a full range of tools and applications to help you with the day-to-day challenges of starting and running a business saving you time and money. Our market leading "Mybusinessworks" online service and "Creditfocus Pro" credit management service are available to our business customers for a small monthly fee. This fee is discounted for Business Start-up customers.

It is easy to arrange an appointment with your Local Business Manager on Freephone 0800 515 462 or alternatively you can apply online at www. barclays.co.uk/business and our New Customer Team will call you and arrange an appointment for you.

To open a business bank account you will need to bring your passport or driving licence or EU national identity card and a utility bill, council tax bill or personal bank statement less than three months old. Depending on your chosen legal status and projected turnover further information may also be required regarding the verification of the business. We will advise you if this is necessary.

During the appointment there will be an opportunity to fully discuss your business idea and the manager will go through the account options available to meet your specific needs.

Having a poor credit record will not necessarily mean that you cannot open a business account. The manager will consider every customer's individual circumstances on their own merit."

In Summary

The reality is that in practice, many start-ups (and established businesses) get into difficulties with cash flow. When receipts of money due into their accounts are paid late, it can cause a shortage of funds in the account. Outgoings, particularly direct debits and standing orders, will not be paid out by the bank if the funds are not available and this can create a vicious circle in which the business fails to pay its creditors and incurs substantial bank charges for the administration work. If a business has a personal business bank manager there is someone to speak to (as opposed to a call centre). They will want the business to succeed and as long as the business has been fair with them, they will help them through such difficult situations, as far as they are authorised to.

Before you start-up, visit the business managers of your local banks and find out what they can offer you. Consider the person you will be dealing with; your local Business Manager. Choose a manager who you feel is approachable and supportive; someone you can "connect" with and create a relationship. After one year you will have established a track record and the bank will want to retain you as a client. Further facilities such as overdrafts and loans which are difficult to attain at the outset will become available to you as a result of proving you can organise your business transactions effectively.

Before the next chapters which relate to the financial sections of business plans, let's look at a business which started over ten years ago and see how Christine Anne Rowland's Beauty & Holistic Therapy business managed to deal with everything we've discussed so far.

Case Study: Christine Anne Rowlands Beauty & Holistic Therapy (Part 1)

Christine started her business in the 1990's with the help of her local Enterprise Agency. She had qualified in holistic therapy and worked for two years at a successful salon where she had been able to practise and add to her professional skills. Whilst employed, she gained experience in how a successful salon was run and when her family encouraged her to start-up herself, she decided to test the market and her own business skills, renting a room in her sister's business premises and offering clients beauty and holistic therapy treatments.

Getting Start-up Help

While she was researching and preparing, before taking the plunge, Christine had found that there were grants of £1000 available for business start-ups in her local area. The grant would only be given on the approval of a viable business plan; training and one-to-one advice was available to assist the applicant with this. Advice and monitoring in the first year of the business was also available. She approached her local Enterprise Agency, attended the business start-up workshops and was then allocated a Business Adviser who worked with her on a one-to-one basis to help her complete a business plan. Christine says she had excellent help with her business planning and recommends that start-ups explore all avenues of current business support. Later when she expanded her business, she had to re-write her business plan and found that her Local Authority/Council also provided advice and support to businesses and that they were very helpful too.

She decided to set up as a sole trader and she still is a sole trader, even though her business has grown and she now has moved to her own larger premises and has two employees. Initially she found the financial aspects of the business daunting and admits that she would have struggled to cope with writing a business plan without considerable help from her Business Adviser and her husband Nigel.

Her daughter worked in business and she started a simple book-keeping system for Christine consisting of two daily lists; the first one was her takings each day and the second one was for her business expenses each day. These records were hand-written and filed in a folder with receipts included at the back of each expense listing. Christine was very meticulous; in fact her Business Adviser told her that she kept her records better than he kept his.

She has had two accountants since she set up; the first accountant was very good and she was very happy with the way he completed her self-assessment return but as her business has grown she has moved to another firm which offers help on all aspects of business, including taking care of her employee wages and tax and national insurance and the legal aspects of employing people. Whilst she still keeps her lists, her daughter now completes the book-keeping on a computerised system which the accountant has recommended, and which can be easily converted to what he needs at year end. Christine has not found the cost to be prohibitive but is aware that without the help from her daughter on the book-keeping side, it would be a lot more expensive.

With regard to registering for VAT, Christine was happy to remain below the threshold until she was confident that she could run the business, although she knows that this is not an option for other businesses who are selling for example, cars and barges (her examples, not sure where the barges came from).

When it came to financing the business, Christine says that because of her maturity and the fact that she had been employed for a long period, she had been able to save money and did not need external borrowing. She also had the benefit of the government grant, which, although it was not a huge amount of money, it did help with her setting up expenses. She could have chosen to borrow and start-up on a grand scale but she chose to rent a room in her sister-in-laws premises at a reasonable cost and kept her start-up expenses to a minimum until she knew the business was likely to be successful and sustainable.

Although she did not need to borrow, she still approached the local banks and "shopped around" for the best deal in opening a business bank account. She was initially given 18 months free banking and has had two business bank accounts over the lifetime of her business. She found that as the business grew and her banking requirements changed, particularly with banking cash and needing a card machine, she could get better terms from a competitor. She asked other business people who they used and using their recommendations arranged a meeting with the local Business Manager at the branch before changing. She recommends that start-up businesses do the same and work it out as you go along, especially by talking to other business people you know and Business Bank Managers.

Business Plans

With regard to business plans, because she had to write one, Christine became familiar with aspects of business she had no idea about and this helped her tremendously when she came into contact with the legal aspects of being in business, especially with regard to working from business premises. When I asked her about Health & Safety (H&S) requirements, she said she "just knew about them" and then realised that this was because at every stage of her training, H&S had been included; when studying for her holistic therapy qualification the relevant parts had been included and when undertaking the start-up business training, it was covered again. Work experience had also given her an insight into the practical aspects of H&S and other legal obligations. Later, when her business grew and she moved to larger premises, she had to re-think her legal requirements and had to produce another business plan in order to get the relevant planning permission and change of use authorisation.

Christine says that there is plenty of support out there for small businesses, although she agrees that grants seem to have all but disappeared. We will look at Christine's business again when we come to the legal aspects of starting a business later in the book.

Chapter 5

Business Plans 1: The Sales Forecast

Making decisions is always easier if the facts and figures are set out in front of you. This is what a business plan does; if you can forecast your sales figures and your expenses, especially month by month to show any seasonal fluctuations, you will have a very good idea as to whether or not your business venture will provide you with enough money to risk you undertaking it. Any investor or financier will do too.

If, when you have bought stock and paid for any other expenses, there is money left over from sales income and you know that is enough for you to manage on, you will feel more confident (and less worried) about taking the plunge. You do not want to be working hard and ending up with nothing to show for it; a lot of people who rent or buy shops and businesses on a whim and without any financial knowledge and skills, end up working long and often boring hours in an outlet with very few customers, and spend that time worrying as to how they are going to pay their bills and loans. For the sake of gaining a small amount of financial know how, you can avoid this.

Writing a Business Plan

A business plan is a story, often with pictures (charts and illustrations) of your business. Having a business plan is a great motivator as it is a way of setting goals and you will now be very aware that if you are looking to borrow money or receive some form of grant, the finance provider will want to see a business plan. Also as they are in effect your financiers, you will need to write the plan in their way.

A bank manager or business adviser will apportion a short time (probably half an hour or less) to reading a plan, taking it in and assessing the information, before making a decision as to whether or not to grant or lend you money. Because of this, business plans have a "format"; they are laid out in a certain way that makes it easy for the reader to assess. Some lenders will expect you to use their specific format so you may have to transfer your information into their business plan template; this is not difficult once you have prepared your information, understood the jargon and decided what they need to know.

Personal information and your profile or CV will be included in a business plan, along with a sales and marketing strategy for the business. As mentioned earlier, this book is centred on the financial and legal aspects of a business start-up and the financial projections are what any lender will look most closely at, so these are the sections we will consider:

The Sales Forecast
The Profit & Loss (P&L) Forecast
The Cash Flow Forecast
The Balance Sheet

The Sales Forecast

The starting point of the financial projections in a business plan is the Sales Forecast (although some business start-ups will complete an expenses forecast first—see later).

A lender will expect you to estimate or "predict" your **sales income**, also called "sales revenue", for at least the first 12 months of your business, month by month, culminating in your annual sales figure or "sales turnover". The reason that lenders want to see the information month by month is because a business needs to take into account the periods when it will be most and least busy; this helps them "plan" around fluctuations. By understanding these variances, often arising because of your customers' buying habits, you will be able to assess when to buy in stock, when to adjust your prices through promotions and discounts, when to get in extra labour and so forth. Each business will be subject to "market trends" and "seasonal variations" and by showing that you have studied the market by looking at statistics, speaking to similar business owners and generally conducting detailed market research, a lender will look on your business plan much more favourably.

When we ask people in business planning workshops to come up with their sales "projections" they are usually horrified; they have no idea how or where to start.

Where to start; selling prices

The easiest way to start is to set your selling prices; this will be a price per product or an hourly, daily or weekly rate for a service, depending on the type of business. Once you have come up with your selling price list, you will need to estimate how many customers you will have and how much they will buy from you, month by month. Let's look at some different types of businesses and how people estimate these sales figures.

The basic rule about setting selling prices is that they must be based on "what the market will bear" or the "going rate". This means that selling prices should always be set at what your particular customers are willing to pay and this will generally be in line with what your local competitors are charging.

Competitors' selling prices

Finding out about your competitors, including their selling prices, is a major part of market research and will help you decide on how to do things in your business. Your selling prices will need to be in line with theirs if you are to compete successfully. As well as the selling prices you will have to look at what you are offering the customer; what exactly are they getting for their money and how can your business match, and improve on what your competitors are giving them.

So, a plumber, joiner, builder or a trainer like myself, would set an hourly rate, a daily rate, a weekly rate, and also learn how to "price contract work" (this could be done by getting a quotation from an existing business in the same area for a similar contract).

Where a business sells products, it involves much more work than setting fees or rates of pay but you still need a price list, sometimes by law, and setting product selling prices in line with those of your closest competitor is the way to start.

Then you will have to estimate the number of customers you will have each month and how much they will buy from you. If you are offering a service, you can start by deciding how many days work there will be for you in a particular month or how many days you will be open for business. Each month will vary—use a business diary to plan the number of days each month; a diary will also enable you to jot down important things as you go along such as vehicle mileage, money you have paid out etc. and is a really valuable thing to have.

Where you are selling products or have an outlet such as a shop, a café, bar or restaurant, to simplify things you can try to find out the average likely spend per customer, rather than costing out each item sold. If you can get the accounts for a similar business which is for sale, that too will give you some indication of a year's sales; you will still have to research sales month by month though in addition.

If you need to borrow finance for your business, the more research you have done and the more realistically you estimate the number of customers you are likely to get, the more favourably a bank manager or business adviser will look upon your sales forecast.

To summarise; your sales forecast, month by month will be predicted by:

- Your average hourly, daily or contract rate multiplied by number of days work in the month for services
- The average number of customers per day at an average sales figure per head—for example, 50 customers spending on average £5 each
- Using the monthly sales figures of a similar business you know or have researched

Formatting the Sales Forecast

To set out the sales forecast for business plan purposes, make 13 columns on a piece of paper and label each one with the month, starting with the month you will commence trading. Underneath each month write down the total monthly value of sales in £'s from your calculations. Add up the 12 months' figures and put the total in the end column—this is your predicted sales turnover for the year.

Seasonal Variations

No business has the same amount of sales in every month of the year and the bank will definitely send you away if you just put the same figure in each month, whatever business you are in. Monthly or seasonal variations in sales are common to all businesses. It is well known in business that January is a poor month for sales as potential customers are cash poor after Christmas (exceptions would be exercise and slimming programmes, do you see where I'm going?) Try to adjust your figures for any such seasonal variations, for example, festive occasions such as Valentine's Day or the run up to Christmas when sales for certain products and services will be higher; months with holidays, particularly school holidays which can significantly affect the sales of some businesses. Good businesses are prepared for "downturn" periods and offer discounts, sales and promotions, to weather the storm of them.

When you have finished your sales forecast, you will have a selling price list and will have predicted customer sales month by month for the first year of your business. You will know when the good times will be and also the bad times; this will encourage you to set aside money to cover the downturns and assist you in surviving.

Sales Forecasts from a lender's perspective

As mentioned earlier, any lender will look closely at your sales projections to check that the sales figures are realistic and achievable. They will do this by assessing how much research you have done into the market, and deciding if there is enough room in that market for your business. If you meet their criteria, they will then want to know why will people buy from you rather than where they buy from at present.

A financier will expect to see detailed monthly sales calculations as background information to the final figures. It is so important to show that you have done enough market research; your whole business plan centres around having as many customers and as many sales as you predict.

Next, you need to forecast the business expenses. You will be pleased to read that this is much easier!

Chapter 6

Business Plans 2: The Profit
& Loss (P&L) Forecast

Forecasting business expenses

Forecasting monthly business expenses is often easier than forecasting sales as the costs can be more accurately estimated. Expenses for premises, for example, can be researched by visiting an estate agent and getting details of the rent, rates, services etc. for an outlet or unit similar to one which would be suitable for your business needs.

Suppliers of stock and providers of equipment, accountants, banks and solicitors will all give you quotes for their services if you ask, and you will be able to research the cost of any other business expenses you need to forecast.

Personal Survival Budget

Finance providers like to see a personal survival budget—a statement of the owner's personal monthly income and expenditure—so that they can estimate how much that person needs to take out of the business each month for their own use. This money is known as "drawings" which are profits taken out of the business for the owner's personal use.

Fixed Costs

If your business is starting out on a mobile basis or if you are working from home, the sales forecast is probably the simpler statement to start with. Where you have substantial "fixed" costs such as rent, rates, wages, loan repayments etc. which have to be paid for every month, it is sometimes better to forecast the business expenses first as you will be able to see how much money in sales income you need to take to cover these expenses, make a wage for yourself and retain some profit as on-going finance.

Fixed costs are those which have to be paid each month whether or not the business makes a profit. It is better to list the fixed costs first when setting out your business expenses because they have to be met each month regardless of sales. Any fixed costs should be considered seriously at start-up; for example, if you are going to borrow money, you will have to meet regular loan repayments and if you get business premises you will have to pay monthly rent and associated costs right from the outset. Similarly, if you employ someone, you will have to pay them regular wages and pay employer's national insurance to HMRC. Because all of these expenses will occur before you make a single sale, finance providers will look at them carefully and assess the ability of your sales to cover them.

Break-even Analysis

For this reason, finance providers use a technique known as "break-even" analysis. Break-even analysis shows the point at which a business makes enough profit from sales to cover its fixed costs. They are interested in this because many people do not realise when they start out just how many sales they will have to make each week before they cover their fixed costs, let alone make a profit which enables them to take their drawings and leave enough in the business to keep it trading.

Calculating the Break-even point

A simple example of how break-even analysis is useful is when a mobile hairdresser or beautician considers renting a room or a chair in a salon, rather than working on a mobile basis. As a mobile technician, they bought products and had transport costs to consider—no fixed costs, costs only occurred when they had a customer and worked. Once they take on premises, they have a monthly rent to pay, a fixed cost they will be liable for even if they do not work. If the rent is only £50 per week, it is still a fixed cost which has to be paid for. Say an average sale for them is £40 and £10 of that is profit after the expenses of £30 have been taken away, it will take the profit from five sales each week to cover the £50 rent; probably one day's work before they cover their fixed expenses.

That is why break-even analysis is important; if profit is low and fixed costs are high, there will have to be a lot of customer sales to cover them. Finance providers will always look at fixed costs and the break-even point closely; they will want to know how you can cover your fixed costs (especially their loan repayment) if you do not get as many customers as you forecast or if for some reason, such as illness, you cannot work in the business.

Profit Margins

Another concept financiers are interested in is "profit margin" which is a measure used by "trading" businesses (those buying and selling goods) to monitor performance. For them, the "Gross Profit" is the amount of profit you make on each sale, after the deduction of "direct costs" and before they pay out any other business expenses. For example, if you sell something on E-bay for £10 and it cost you £5, you have made a Gross Profit of £5.

This is shown in a forecast as follows:

Sales	£10
Cost of Sales	£5
Gross Profit	£5

If yours is a trading business, finance providers like to see the gross profit figure as a percentage and to calculate this you divide the Gross Profit by the Sales figure and multiply the result by 100—in this case £5 /£10 *100 = 50% profit margin.

Measuring profit margins is very important for businesses that manufacture or sell products as it indicates how well they are trading; if you buy and sell well, your margin will reflect this. When prices from your suppliers go up or you pay more for your manufacturing, profit margins go down and these are important indicators for trading businesses which should be continuously monitored.

Selling Services: Indirect Costs / Overheads

Where people sell services rather than products, there are often no direct costs and therefore no profit margin to manage. For example, a financial adviser or a book-keeper does not usually have direct costs; they will have "indirect" costs such as travel, stationery, computers etc. often classified as "overheads". Their sales are sometimes described as "fees" and their expenses are listed below the fees then deducted to give a "Net Profit". There is no Cost of Sales or Gross Profit in their forecast as they are selling services as opposed to trading (and therefore have no need to calculate or manage a Gross Profit margin).

Formatting the Profit & Loss Forecast

When you have estimated your annual business expenses and broken them down into monthly fixed or variable costs, you are ready to complete your Profit & Loss forecast, again thirteen columns, one for each month and an annual total.

For traders, the Sales Forecast you have prepared is the top line of the P&L Account Forecast followed by the Cost of Sales (the stock figure necessary each month to fulfil your sales). Deducting your Cost of Sales figure each month from the Sales will give you the third line, the Gross Profit. This is the money you have made from buying and selling or trading and is used in the profit margin calculation.

Businesses selling services will just transfer their forecast sales to the P&L Forecast and follow them with the monthly expenses which are detailed line by line into categories appropriate to the business, for example, rent, rates, services, wages, administration, motor vehicle etc.

For either business, when the expenses are added together and deducted from the monthly sales or gross profit, you will have calculated your monthly and annual "Net Profit" (also known as "the bottom line").

Reality check

At this point you will be able to consider the viability of your business proposition, that is, undertake a reality check on your business idea. The net profit is what you will end up with each month before you take any drawings. By comparing this with your personal survival budget you will be able to assess whether or not the net profit will be enough to pay you the drawings you need to take out and enable you to leave the remainder in the business to keep it afloat. It will also assist anyone involved in the financing of the business to see that the business will be profitable enough.

Let's return to Christine Anne Rowlands and look at how she weighed up the financial situation when, later in her business career, she considered moving from renting a room to having her own much larger and substantially more expensive business premises.

Case Study: Christine Anne Rowlands Beauty & Holistic Therapy (Part 2)

As Christine's client base grew and her business became more established, she reached the stage where she had to make some serious financial decisions. The business had outgrown the space as she was retaining and gaining clients and they were asking for additional treatments. This meant that if she wanted to take her business forward, she would have to move to bigger premises and employ someone to deliver these additional treatments. She discovered that residential premises were available further along the road from where she rented her room and she enquired about taking them over. The landlord was keen for her to go ahead but she would need to contact the local authority with regard to planning permission for the change of use of the premises from residential to business use. On contacting the Local Authority she found that they would need to see a revised business plan for her business before permission could be granted.

She sat down again with her husband, Nigel (Christine felt that the move was so big that she needed another view and some support—she recommends getting help from reliable and knowledgeable people before making such far reaching business decisions) and together they calculated the cost of the move and forecast the future monthly on-going expenses. Then they added a further 20% as a safety net to the figures!

Once the expenses had been forecast, Christine was easily able to work out how many new client sales and increased sales from existing clients she would have to make to cover the costs. As she did not immediately need all of the additional space, her initial thoughts were to let one of the rooms to a nail technician who would offer the additional treatments that her customers were requesting. She was taking on two floors of a building and as she did not intend to convert the whole of the two floors immediately, there would be an extra room on Christine's floor which could be sub-let and the rental income would contribute to the additional expenses. As taking on an employee at this stage was too much of a financial (and legal) commitment alongside the move to new premises, she decided to look to letting the room to someone who also worked on a self-employed basis.

Her story shows how she went about successfully expanding her business in a controlled way and you can probably see now why producing or revising a P&L Forecast is so important when changes happen in your business. If your business idea or your expansion is not going to be profitable, you do not want to go ahead with it. Even if it is profitable, it then needs sufficient capital and cash to keep it going over time. For this reason, potential investors need the P&L Forecast to be adjusted for cash fluctuations, which leads us to the next statement necessary in a business plan, the Cash Flow Forecast.

Chapter 7

Business Plans 3: The Cash Flow Forecast

"Cash is King!"

The Profit & Loss Forecast gives you and other interested parties an insight into how your business is likely to perform in the first year. The better the research, the more realistic the forecast will be, so outlining your sales in detail is important and worth taking time over. However, being profitable is not enough in business. If your business runs out of cash before your profits start coming in, you will not be able to continue to trade and because of this, lenders of finance are usually more interested in a Cash Flow Forecast than in a P&L Forecast.

How is the Cash Flow Forecast (CFF) different from the P&L Forecast?

A Cash Flow Forecast is different from a P&L Forecast in that it shows month by month how the "cash" flows into and out of the business, rather than when income from sales is earned or expenses are incurred.

For example, if a business offers "credit" to its customers in line with its competitors and the sales made in January are not paid for until March, the business will be unable to fund the expenses in January and February from sales income. In a P&L Forecast the sale would be recorded when it took place in January but in a Cash Flow Forecast it would be recorded in March, when the money for the sale comes into the business bank account. The Cash Flow Forecast highlights delayed sales income and shows clearly where there will be negative cash flow (when expenses exceed sales income) to be managed.

Certain expenses, such as rent, which are recorded monthly in the P&L Forecast, may have to be paid in advance, and before sales income can cover them; this can also lead to cash shortages. Where businesses have high start-up costs or if they sell goods or services on credit to their customers but have to pay for stock in advance, they will need to plan ahead for cash flow imbalances.

A business will always have these cash flow fluctuations; even businesses that do not offer credit may have to wait for payment from their customers after having delivered the goods or services. You can send out an invoice for goods or services which the customer has agreed to pay for within a certain timeframe, but they will often pay late, and as a start-up business there is little you can do about it. You can complain but there are lots of other people out there offering the same products or services and your customer may choose to go elsewhere if they get better terms, i.e. a longer time to pay their invoices.

For all of these reasons, lenders will always be more interested in a Cash Flow Forecast rather than a Profit& Loss Forecast.

Working Capital

"Working capital" is money used to provide for the fluctuations and imbalances in cash flow in the daily running of a business; it is used to manage the peaks and troughs of incomings and outgoings. Whilst you are waiting for payments to come in from customers, you have to carry on making payments for stock and your business expenses and without a backdrop of money to call on you will not survive. Lack of adequate working capital is one of the main reasons businesses fail to grow, and why so many fail to survive within the first 18 months. A Cash Flow Forecast will show you when your outgoings are at their highest in comparison with your incomings and this will enable you to organise corrective action such as using a bank overdraft, where money is lent to you as and when you need it and interest is only charged when the overdraft is used. Other methods of raising short-term finance are available and by planning for cash shortfalls, even if it means using credit cards (carefully and responsibly), you will stay in business.

Christine Anne Rowlands experienced cash flow problems when she moved to her own premises, even though she had carefully researched the costs and revised her business plan. From the start, Christine had made the decision that she would use high quality, branded products for her treatments. These were expensive and as a new customer, the product manufacturers were unwilling to offer credit terms; they expected to be paid up-front on a "pro-forma" basis and she was committed to purchasing a certain level of stock initially, varying from 500 to 1000 units, if she wanted to hold the brands. Sometimes the minimum order of stock was quoted in £'s, especially nail products (the new market Christine was entering into) and her main supplier had a £450 minimum initial order price. Other suppliers accepted smaller orders but all of them had to be paid "upfront" and these additional costs had been missed when revising her business plan. At this stage, she had to break into her 20% safety net figure; without it, she would not have been able to introduce the new products and services.

In conclusion, the P&L Forecast is often the easier statement for you to attempt to produce and therefore the starting point. "Tweaking" your P&L Forecast will then enable you to produce a Cash Flow Forecast and this is the one you and your financiers will use as your operational plan.

Chapter 8

Business Plans 4: The Balance Sheet

The Balance Sheet was once considered to be an integral part of a business plan for start-ups, but less emphasis is placed on it now. The main areas of focus at start-up are often seen as sales generation, profitability and cash flow and for this reason many business plan templates do not include a balance sheet.

Understanding a balance sheet does however make a hugely positive difference to serious business people. It impacts on how they invest in their business, grow it and re-invest, to create their own personal wealth.

Assets and Liabilities

A balance sheet is a statement of the "assets" and "liabilities" of the business at any particular point in time. Put simply, a balance sheet shows:

What the business owns (assets) and what the business owes (liabilities).

The difference between the assets and the liabilities is the owner's capital investment in the business; their "stake" in the business or what it owes to them. Watching your capital investment grow as you work hard in your business is extremely motivating and encourages owners to re-invest and minimise their drawings so that the assets grow continuously.

Growing your Balance Sheet

Financial experts will encourage you to grow your balance sheet as a way to growing your wealth; to get rich. An example of how this works would be where the business buys property (an asset) and takes on a mortgage or loan to pay for it (a liability). As the mortgage or loan is paid, the liability is reduced. The asset remains the same or grows in value and the balance sheet tips to the asset side, thereby increasing the wealth of the business and the owner's stake or capital investment. Using profit to repay the debt, rather than taking it out and spending it, grows a balance sheet and the wealth of the business and its owner.

Balance Sheet divisions

In a formal balance sheet, the assets and liabilities are separated into the following categories:

Fixed Assets (these are long-term with a lifetime of longer than 1 year such as buildings and equipment)

Current Assets (short-term items with a lifetime of less than 1 year such as debtors and cash)

Long Term Liabilities (those having a lifetime of longer than 1 year for example mortgages and the owner's investment)

Current Liabilities (short-term debts to creditors; also bank overdrafts which can be called in at any time)

Liquidity

The reason for the split into time periods is to show the "liquidity" of the business; the ease with which assets can be turned into cash to pay off debts.

As a business grows, lenders will want to look at a balance sheet because it shows clearly the present position of a business in terms of investment and solvency; for start-ups it has less relevance as the assets and liabilities are generally smaller. Nevertheless, if you can master the understanding of it, it will be of great use in managing and growing your business.

Chapter 9

Legal Aspects of Starting a Business

It will be clear by now that working for yourself or starting a business means that you become responsible for much more than when you were working for an employer; in fact, you become responsible for everything. If your business grows and you yourself become an employer, you will have to take care of your employees as well as the business. As well as ensuring that you cover all of the legal aspects of employing people, you will have to calculate and deduct tax and national insurance from their wages and send the money to HMRC and you will have to make sure that the correct insurances for the business and the employees who represent it are in place.

Business Insurances

Anyone who works for themselves can be sued; they have legal responsibilities under the law, including adhering to Health & Safety regulations and meeting the requirements of Trading Standards, and can be taken to court if they fail to comply with the various laws relating to their business. A business selling food can be sued if a customer suffers illness which they claim was a result of eating what they bought; a solicitor, accountant or financial adviser can be sued for giving wrong advice; and a plumber can be sued if a washing machine he has serviced suddenly stops working.

As a business person you are open to complaints and disputes which can lead to legal action and because of this you need to cover any claims by having the appropriate insurances in place. You may never need to use them, but you must have them to protect yourself and the business.

Types of Business Insurance

Business insurance generally falls into two categories:

Professional Indemnity Insurance, relating to insurance cover for professional advisers

Public Liability (including product liability) insurance covering the business relationship with the public

Business insurance offers protection when a lawsuit is brought against you; for example, if someone trips over uneven flooring in your premises and injures themself or claims to have contracted an illness after eating your food product they may see a solicitor and take you to court for failing to fulfil your legal obligations.

Where do people go for business insurance?

Banks, high street brokers, internet websites and professional or trade associations are where most business owners purchase insurance from. If you use your bank, broker or a trade association of which you are a member to purchase business insurance, you will probably be able to get advice on the different products available and help in deciding which policy is best for your business. If you buy from the internet, you will obviously have to look at the specification closely yourself to make sure it covers all eventualities in relation to your business. When you buy from banks, brokers and trade associations, the chances are that it will have been carefully checked by them to ensure it meets the criteria necessary to cover you particular trade, profession or industry, so even if it costs more, it will probably save you time and money in the long term.

Business insurance may not be as expensive as you think; for many start-ups it will range from £150 to £250 per year and can often be paid for in instalments. High risk businesses where claims are likely to be expensive will obviously have higher premiums; scaffolding businesses are an example of this.

Informing existing insurance providers

As well as business insurance you will need to consider your current insurances for your home and motor vehicle. If you fail to tell your existing providers that you are using your home and vehicle for business purposes, if or when you have a claim, they may not pay out. Reputable insurance companies should not charge you a fortune for adding business use to your current insurance policies; if there is a significant increased risk though, such as leaving tools overnight in a vehicle whilst working away, there will probably be an increased charge and conditions attached to the policy.

Other interested parties

As well as your home insurance, when you work from home you are legally obliged to notify your mortgage provider or landlord and the local authority you pay your council tax to. Again additional premiums or business rates will only be applied where there is good reason, usually, increased perceived risk on their part. Each provider will have their own terms; for most start-ups there will be no change, but you should check with them in order to avoid potential future disputes.

Health & Safety (H&S) Legislation

Health & Safety legislation applies to anyone who works for themself and they can be taken to court if they do not comply with it. Having appropriate insurances in place and setting up a mechanism which will keep you in touch with any legal changes on the horizon, will enable you to get on with developing your business. There will be however, be certain areas of H&S legislation which relate specifically to your type of business and you may need specialist advice in this area.

Risk Assessment

In order to comply with Health & Safety legislation, businesses undertake a "risk assessment", which is basically about providing written answers to the following question:

"What could go wrong?"

The government website www.hse.gov.uk gives you access to the latest legislation and you can download a template to create your own H&S policy here.

BIFs & BOPs

General information about the legalities of running a business, including those specific to your industry sector can be obtained from Business Information Factsheets (BIFs) and Business Opportunity Profiles (BOPs).

These are specialist factsheets from a central database which are obtained by some of the banks and start-up business organisations under licence. If your local bank or Enterprise Agency can get these for you, they will act as a useful guide to accessing information from professional and trade associations which will be particularly relevant and helpful in running your business.

Business Contracts

Taking specialist advice before signing contracts and legal agreements such as leases for rented premises is often necessary for new businesses as they need to be aware of any hidden liabilities included in the agreement.

Leasing premises

Areas to check include:

- Length of term. This is the length of the lease in terms of years and months that you are committed to under the agreement. You need to consider this carefully as if your business does not take off as you expect it to you will be paying rent for premises you no longer use. On the other hand, if you are very successful and you have only signed up for say one year, you may have to re-negotiate with the landlord and possibly suffer an increase in rental charges.

  This is a difficult consideration when you start out but there are a lot of business premises for rent and you should be able to negotiate a flexible deal with a responsible landlord. Decide what would be best for your business and negotiate with him or her. Maybe an early "break clause" could be incorporated into the contract or a means of extending the contract under the same terms would be possible after a pre-determined lengths of time, if the landlord is sympathetic to your position as a start-up. As with all contracts you should aim for a "win/win" situation where both parties feel happy with what has been decided.

- Responsibility for repairs and insurance.

  You need to be absolutely clear about who is responsible for what in terms of leased or rented premises. Some landlords include buildings insurance in the rental fee but you need to know how this relates to your business; for example, is your property on the premises insured? The landlord may pay for the insurance of the building, but not the contents. What about public liability—would you be covered under their insurance if someone had an accident there?

- Payments in addition to rent including VAT, service charges, business rates, utilities etc.

  There are sometimes additional payments such as "service charges" which may be payable for leased premises. These tend to cover insurance and the general upkeep and maintenance of premises and may be additional to the rental payment.

  Similarly check that the landlord has given you the full annual rental charge. Ask, for example, is VAT included in the price you have been given if it is payable. Consider who is responsible for paying the business insurance, rates, water and gas and electricity bills for the premises as these costs will have to be found by you if they are not included.

If you are not clear about any of the above and the landlord is unwilling to discuss the lease with you, then you will need to get specialist advice from a solicitor. As with all legal matters, prevention is better than cure!

Contracts, Terms & Conditions (T's & C's) of Business Agreements

Many contracts do not have to be in writing but it is often better if they are as you will have more certainty and evidence of terms you have agreed with your customers and suppliers. Examples of contract situations include:

- Buying & Selling Goods & Services.

  It is always better to have clear terms and conditions attached to any sale you make. In the simplest instance, for example, what is your returns policy? What about complaints procedures, deposits, length of time before payment etc.?

  If these are clearly and simply laid out it will make for a smoother running of your business. You can look at the terms and conditions of a similar business to yours and see what they put forward to get some idea of what yours should be. People like to be clear about exactly what they are getting from you so it is another win/win situation if you take the time to set these out.

- Hiring and buying equipment on credit.

  As with leases for business premises, hiring goods and equipment to enable you to run your business will have contractual obligations; the T's & C's. Businesses often come across problems in this area when they rent vehicles or equipment, for example, cars, vans or lifting equipment such as fork lift trucks. You should go through the contract thoroughly and understand what you are committing the business to. Common problems are early repayment penalties which occur if you return the equipment before the term of the contract has expired and "balloon" payments at the end of the contract should you decide to keep the equipment for longer. It needs to be clear as to who has ownership of and responsibility for the equipment at any stage of the contract. Reading the small print is time consuming but essential, as hire purchase contracts are usually for expensive pieces of machinery and consequences can be costly if you get it wrong.

- General automatic implied laws, for example, the Sale of Goods Act.

The law seeks to protect customers and the Trading Standards Institute www.tradingstandards.gov.uk is there to enforce the law, so you must comply with their requirements. For example, goods must be of "merchantable quality" and if a customer finds that what they bought from you is not properly made and they wish to return it, you must give them their money back. Information on trading standards is easy to obtain; the government body will issue you with a pack of information relating to your specific business, on request. The website has a lot of business information including Consumers/Buyers Rights, Food and Safety regulations and much more.

Franchise and licensing agreements

Companies such as McDonalds, Kwik-Fit, Spar and Subway offer their expertise by selling their successful business models to outlets operating in the same industry as them, through franchise agreements.

A franchise agreement is arranged between the franchisor (say McDonalds) and the franchisee (you) and sets out the terms and conditions of a legal agreement, which entitles you to use their business model of advertising, their suppliers, and their administration systems, for which you will pay an annual amount of money.

Franchising gives you access to proven expertise which helps when starting a new business; from a legal point of view, you do need to get specialist advice before embarking on such an undertaking as you are committing yourself to serious monthly/annual repayments and commitments.

Intellectual Property Rights (IPR) including: Copyright—Trade Marks—Design Rights—Patents—Confidentiality

This can be a very complex and confusing subject and the government provides information and guidance at www.ipo.gov.uk

"ACID" (Anti Copying in Design) is a trade association which can also help as a deterrent to would be infringers of IPR www.acid.eu.com

Innovation and new product development is exciting for everyone, including the government. "Leading edge" products and technology often result in producing high profits for the business owner(s) and high revenues from subsequent taxation into the government coffers. Because of this, business people want to protect their innovation and look to patents, copyright etc. to do this for them. There is help through the government in this area but you have to find a specialist adviser and you will only get significant help if your product or service is seen by them as unique too.

In reality, patents and copyright, although they are important, do not mean that your product or service will not be copied. It means that you can take legal action against the offending business for copying and ask, through the Law Courts, for it to be stopped. This is an expensive and time consuming process and if your new product or service continues to be copied by others, you will probably not be able to afford to keep suing people. Sometimes you have to leave things to market forces, hoping that you make a considerable profit in the early days when your offering is unique and you can charge a high price for it. You can retain customers then through excellent service.

Business Names, Copyright and Intellectual Property Rights

When choosing a name for your business, the legal precedent you need to be aware of relates to "passing off". Passing off is using the name and imagery of an existing business, in a manner that could take trade away from them. For example, if you set up a food outlet and make it look like a McDonalds restaurant (even if you do not use the exact name) they would take you to court to stop you trading; as we know from looking at franchises earlier, you have to pay an annual fee to use their branding and copy their business model and it is against the law to operate as one of their chains without entering into a legal agreement with them.

The danger of being sued under "passing off" means that you will have to check your business name, logo and imagery to ensure they are not already in use. Banks "Google" business names to check that the name of a new business is not already in use, before opening a new business bank account. If the name is already in use, you cannot open an account in it.

When you have got your business name, then other businesses will not be able to use it as they could be considered to be "passing off", but it will be up to you to stop them doing this. You do not have to be a limited company to prevent others using your business name once you have set up; sole traders are entitled to the same rights under the law.

Employment & Staff Issues

This area has many potential and costly pitfalls. Business owners employing staff need to have up to date information on employment law and employee rights. Processes for hiring staff including job descriptions, interviewing, gathering references and providing employment contracts have to be thorough to prevent legal problems. Information can be obtained from www.emplaw.co.uk and www.acas.org.uk

There are also helpful publications which are either free or moderately priced but taking on an employee is a serious step in the growth of a business in terms of legal obligations; to comply with employees' rights it often means that when you take on employees, you will need to have access to a Human Resources specialist or a legal firm which specialises in employment law. If you get it wrong it will be extremely costly.

Taking on employees will be essential as your business grows but in the early stages it is sensible to use sub-contract or flexible arrangements until you are certain that there is enough business to be able to meet the financial and legal obligations of taking on employees. As with any other aspect of growing your business, there will come a time when you will have to use (paid) external advisers and only you will be able to decide when this is.

Although the legal side of starting a business is a potential minefield, people do get through it successfully and keeping up to date with new rules and legislation is part of business. Getting regular newsletters from responsible bodies (and reading them!) such as your local accountant will keep you informed of changes, as will joining a business network such as the Chamber of Commerce where you can meet regularly with other people in a similar position and share views. Health & Safety regulations and general government "red-tape" change continually and ignorance of the changes is no defence if you are taken to court by say, Trading Standards.

Case Study: Christine Anne Rowlands Beauty & Holistic Therapy (Part 3)

When Christine moved from her rented room to her own premises (further along the road but covering two floors of a three storey building) she found she had many more legal responsibilities to consider.

Leasing business premises

After revising and updating the financial aspects of her business plan, Christine was then faced with the legal aspects of leasing her own premises. The terms of the lease and rental agreement had to be thoroughly reviewed at the outset. This included negotiating on the length of time it covered (too short or long a lease has implications which each business has to consider based on their objectives). Christine had heard of a start-up business in the same locality where the business owner arrived for work one day and saw a "For Sale" notice on the building he had his office in. His lease allowed the owner of the building to sell at any time and he had not considered the effect of this on his business. It made her realise that when renting her premises, the terms of the lease needed to be clear and agreed by both parties in order to avoid interruption to the business. She studied the lease agreement carefully and then agreed the length of time and rental payments with subsequent dates for revision with the landlord who had them incorporated into the contract before she signed.

Insurances

With regard to insurance for the premises, the lease stated that the landlord had responsibility for all external aspects of the business premises and she was responsible for internal ones. For her insurance cover to be effective she then had to look at the terms and conditions in detail and ensure she complied with them; otherwise the insurance company would refuse to pay out on any claim.

Having the best and most appropriate insurances is essential in Christine's business. She has to have insurance cover for the following:

- Contents insurance for her business premises (the landlord is responsible for external aspects of the building under the terms of the lease)
- Public Liability insurance, to cover the cost of any claims which might be brought against her for accidents on her premises
- Employer Liability insurance, to cover the cost of any legal action an employee may bring against her
- She has also told her car insurers that she uses her vehicle for business use (this does not cost any more but would cover her if, for example, she was involved in an accident whilst travelling to her suppliers on business).

Christine is particularly careful about choosing her insurer and has specialist insurance through the Federation of Holistic Therapists. Her qualifications were awarded by this professional body and she has retained her membership which entitles her to purchase their high-quality insurance at a very competitive price. Federations, professional and trade associations often offer their members products and services which are beneficial to their specific businesses which Christine says often make it well worth the membership fees.

Planning permission & Local Authority conditions

As the premises had been residential, she had to apply to the local authority for change of use to business. This involved several meetings with their officers and the updating of her business plan. There were conditions she had to adhere to with regard to the conversion of the premises, for example, providing disabled access. She learned that neon signs were prohibited and that opening hours were limited (not after 8pm or Sundays) because of the location in a residential area. Her "A" board for advertising would not be allowed outside the premises as it was a public footpath (Christine later got round this by locating hers on the grass verge on the other side of the path). Throughout the conversion of the premises, she was inspected regularly to ensure that she was complying with regulations and although Christine found this demanding in terms of trips down to the Town Hall, she says that the people were extremely helpful towards her.

Licences & other legal obligations

Once the lease was sorted and the conversion had been accepted she then looked inwards into the legal necessities which would ensure her insurance was effective. She found that several licences were needed including the following:

- She had to register with the Environmental Health Department of the local authority in order to be able to use needles (for electrolysis treatments). There was an initial cost for the licence and a subsequent annual fee.
- To play CD's in the treatment rooms, she needed a music licence to comply with the broadcasting and performing rights regulations; if she used her computer to watch television on she would also need a television licence too. She later found that there were spa CD's that could be bought and used without the licence, as the artists were not from the performing rights society.
- Her electrical appliances had to be Portable Appliance Tested (PAT) initially and every three years after.
- She had to keep an accident book (in case claims were brought against her at a later date).
- Her data had to be securely saved to ensure client confidentiality.

Employing staff

Although when Christine revised her business plan, she had not intended to employ staff, she now has two employees. Moving to her own premises and employing staff have been serious decisions for Christine and she was determined that she would ensure she had enough customers before she embarked on taking these steps.

Her first employee was a family member, her daughter, and she says because she trusted her, it made it easier to take such a big step. Her customer base was growing and she had larger premises so although she did not set out purposely to employ anyone, the fact that her daughter wanted to work with her made it easy.

Her second employee was the nail technician who rented a room from her. She had operated on a self-employed basis until family commitments meant that she was struggling to promote and manage her business and decided to look for employed part-time work. She approached Christine with her decision and as Christine knew by this time that the customers for nails were growing and that the nail technician was likeable and reliable, she decided to employ her on a part-time basis, rather than have her leave.

With regard to the legal side of employing people, Christine's new accountant takes care of it. If she is unsure of anything she telephones him and he will signpost her to where she can get the relevant information if he does not have it. Like all employers she found it a big step in her business career but knows that it was carefully thought through and necessary to grow her business.

Business names

Christine thought about business names when she was starting up. She spent a lot of time looking for an appropriate name for her business and kept finding that the ones she liked were already in use. During the process of searching for a name, a family member asked her what was wrong with using her own name. She was finally convinced when he mentioned that using his own name seemed good enough for Alan Sugar and so it would presumably be good enough for her. So Christine Anne Rowlands: Beauty &Holistic Therapy was created, and continues to go from strength to strength.

Chapter 10

Management Information Systems (MIS)

As businesses grow, the owner will have to employ people to cope with the extra work. When this happens it becomes much more difficult for them to know exactly what is happening in the business. The owner may employ a salesperson, an accounts person, a distribution person and so forth—whoever they need to take some of the work from them as more customers come along and it becomes difficult for them to do everything themselves. When this happens, it is easy to lose control of your business. When it was just you, you knew everything that was happening in your business and out in the market. Once other people become involved in the operation of your business, it is important to maintain this control yet delegate responsibility to others.

Effective delegation to other people involves setting out what you want from them and their reporting back to you what happened in practice. Because of this, growing business develop Management Information Systems (MIS) which contain detailed information relating to the performance of each area of the business.

These systems do exactly what the name suggests; they give the owner management information, which in turn allows him or her to retain control of the business, especially in the areas they have delegated to others.

Setting up a system

Management information should be produced and discussed regularly; most businesses have monthly, fortnightly or weekly meetings where the information is discussed and plans are made to move forward from the information. Along with financial information such as the Profit & Loss Account, there should be other information included (other measurements of progress) which is equally important in the running of the business such as the following:

- Product sales information—often broken down into product lines or categories which enable the business to find the best and worst selling lines
- Stock and distribution information—on time or late deliveries; stock shortages or excesses; any relevant supplier information such as increased charges or discounts
- Marketing information—number of enquiries; conversion of enquiries to sales; returns by product category; number of new customers; number of repeat customers; competitor information; advertising costs and measurements of success

At the start of your business, such detailed information would have taken a lot of your time which could probably have been utilized in a more effective way but as your business grows, setting up a MIS will give you a clearer indication of how well your business is actually doing in specific terms and most importantly, it will enable you to delegate effectively. At a basic level you need to know what sells best and which areas make most profit. Setting up a customer database (even just a manual list of customers and their contact details—if they give it to you willingly and you safeguard it, you will not be guilty of contravening Data Protection rules) will enable you to focus on them, keep in touch with them and get that all important repeat business.

Secure storage of information

Holding information carries responsibilities. One of the reasons businesses fail is because they lose their information. When you start-up you have a lot of information in your head and you start to record it because you simply can't remember it all when you need to access it. Backing up recorded information should be a routine and a priority as you will lose time and money if it is lost and cannot be retrieved.

Internet systems using the "cloud" provide an up to date method of backing up computerised data. They can be downloaded easily and even if you have to pay for a system, like insurance, it will be worth it. Through encryption your data is secured and this means you will comply with Data

Protection regulations covering the holding of personal information. If your business is not computerised you will have to use safe facilities for the storage of such information. Recent stories in the news of computer hackers stealing customer data have shown that if you lose the respect of your customers in this way, you will lose your business too. If your business is not computerised you will have to use safe facilities for storage of such information.

Unless you are an accountant or a marketer, it is unlikely that you will be able to set up an all-singing, all-dancing set of management information but you can and should, set up a simple recording system, say on a spread sheet, which will keep you adequately informed on performance in your key areas. Just decide what this key information is for your business and design a simple layout and use it regularly. There is a well-known saying in business: "Don't expect what you don't inspect". Management information systems are essential if you delegate; they keep the business on (your) track.

Chapter 11

And finally . . .

By now you have enough information about starting-up in business to assist you in deciding if taking your business idea further, stepping out onto the self-employed route or actually setting up a small business is what you really want and feel capable of doing. Even if it is not your first choice and you would prefer to be employed, you are now aware of the basic financial and legal facts relating to self-employment and can use this option as a stepping stone to landing that great job, eventually.

It is important to remember that you will learn as you go along; you know how to get started and where to look for further help and advice.

A recession can be the perfect time for starting up in business as the market (people with money to spend) are looking for alternatives that offer great value for money. If you can find a gap, where the competition has gone out of business or standards have slipped, it could be the perfect opportunity for you to make your entrance.

This book is your foundation in building a business, so don't stop here. Go to the agencies and get as much help and advice as possible and keep up with everything on the legal side. "Test" before you commit your precious resources; this will help you to find out how to sell yourself and your products and services, and enable you to learn and adjust as you go along.

Have the magic formula "Sales-Expenses = Profit/Loss" firmly imprinted on the inside of your forehead for when you have to make financial business decisions and watch your cash flow continuously.

If having a business or working for yourself is your dream, you now know how to go about it; so step-up, start-up and stay-up! Good luck with your venture and thank you for reading this book; I hope it has informed, motivated and inspired you to move your business idea forward.